LIVE TO TELL AGAIN

TALES OF SELF-DISCOVERY AND HEALING

BRANDON SPARS

D1445314

WAYZGOOSE PRESS

Edited by Maggie Sokolik

Cover design by DJ Rogers for Book Branders

This volume is dedicated to my beloved wife because she always believes in me even when I don't.
I love you, Irma.

CONTENTS

PREFACE

What is a Brandon Spars? Well, first off, he's at least eight feet tall. You can't tell by looking at him if he's entertaining. Some people look like they have interesting stories to tell. Some look like they may work in finance. Brandon sorta leans toward the finance side. Or a high-school teacher, which makes sense, because he *is* a high school teacher. But that just adds to his mystique.

So many of his stories are about adventure, mishap and getting out into the wild that there is immediately a wonderful tension when Brandon begins talking. You can't help but ask yourself, "Should a guy who might be an actuary even go outside? I don't think this is a good idea. Is he wearing sunscreen?" And then you're hooked. Because you gotta know if he's going to live through it.

Brandon tells a story about getting sent to Jakarta, or Sumatra, or Makassar, or one of those places that make me think of giant spiders, to be a teacher in a jungle village. But when he gets there, everybody has disappeared into the jungle, with no forwarding address—everybody but one old man whose entire English vocabulary is, "Hello. I love you." Obviously, if you are only going to know four English words, those are a pretty good selection.

So Brandon spends several months (a year?) alone in the jungle save for the old man. Conversations are limited. There's not much dialogue. It might not sound like a very interesting story. But that's the thing about Brandon, he mines the amazing out of the mundane. He finds the best AND the worst in situations and helps his listeners, and readers, understand how sweet life is precisely because we get our share of best and worst. Brandon quickly and engagingly draws the links that explain how tragedy can lead to joy if you are willing keep trudging on.

I stand on stage for a living, and if you stand on stage a lot, that means you are in the wings of a lot of theaters listening to, and watching, a lot of other entertainers. I learned long ago that you can't judge how a person will act on stage by the way they act off stage. I mean, I'm funny on stage but I don't look funny. Which isn't to say that I'm not funny looking- I just don't look funny. In fact, people tell me all the time that I look tired or angry. My response is that I am tired of people telling me I look angry. But anyway, this about Brandon. He doesn't look angry or tired. In fact, he looks curious. And curious is good. He steps out in the world not begrudging that he has to run this errand, or complete that task- he steps outside wondering what marvelous or amazing thing will happen this time.

So, sit back with this book and prepare yourself for the ups and downs of an everyday guy who views the world from two feet higher up than you, and thus delivers a perspective you've never imagined.

Bil Lepp
Halfdollar, West Virginia

Bil Lepp is an American storyteller and a five-time winner of the West Virginia State Liars' Contest. He performs at storytelling festivals around the nation and is a regular performer at the National Storytelling Festival in Jonesborough, Tennessee.

PART I
THE STORYTELLING

INTRODUCTION

*L*ive to Tell Again is the second volume in this series. The first volume (*Live to Tell*) has received positive feedback from both teachers and storytellers, which prompted me to hurry up and get the second volume out. It focuses on "true stories" as a genre of tale-telling, much like fairytales are a genre. I have engaged in many interesting discussions about what "true" means when it comes to telling "true stories" at the Moth or other venues. I would recommend that any interested readers of this volume read the introduction to the first volume to understand the distinction I make between "true stories" and "factual stories."

Live to Tell has proved especially useful in the classroom. So far, I am aware that the book has been used successfully in middle school, high school, and college, as well as classrooms for the subjects of ESL, theater, and literature.

I have used the book myself for ESL classes at UC Berkeley Summer English Language Studies, and the visiting international students love being able to read the scripts for the stories before watching the videos (all at brandonspars.com).

The scripts help them prepare for watching the performances, enabling them to look up vocabulary they might not be immediately familiar with. Then, they complete activities in which they predict where the storyteller might become more animated or rapid in pace, where there might be pauses, where there might be sound effects—all the unspoken, nuanced elements of using a language. Students are excited to see how accurate they were in their predictions.

In a summer camp for middle school students, I used the book in a similar way to practice not only natural language but to work directly on the performance aspects of storytelling.

This second volume provides more material for teachers who enjoyed using the first one. I anticipate that this volume will have some additional uses, since it focuses on the use of storytelling for two specific purposes: self-discovery and healing.

The first two tales are about significant moments in my life when I made big changes. The first was at college where I had begun pre-med studies and then moved to chemistry. I had loved chemistry all of my life, and my father, who was a chemical engineer, would bring home glassware to add to our home laboratory. One of my most exciting childhood memories was when my father blew up the laboratory. It was just a small hydrogen explosion, but I still remember how a broken piece of glassware got embedded deep into the ceiling drywall.

But my love of storytelling was churning within me, and eventually it led to a crisis. In the introduction of the first volume, I mention how I took a term off from school and traveled out to my family's cabin on the Gasconade River. It was there that my grandfather regaled me with tales throughout my childhood—not folktales or fairy tales, but tales about the river where we were; tales that were meant to be taken as "true." It was also there in our cabin on the river that I redirected my life away from the sciences and into the fuzzier world of literature and story-telling. The river became my muse, and most of my first stories were about it.

The second story is about how I became a teacher. I ultimately graduated from college with a degree in English, and at that particular time in life, I was sure I wanted to be a writer. I thought writing literature was a higher calling than simply telling oral tales. I imagined myself sipping an espresso, having just finished a large manuscript; or I would picture myself collapsing in a large bed in a ware-house somewhere having stayed up three days straight writing.

This romantic vision of myself as a writer, interestingly enough, never included my sitting down to do the hard work of actual writing. And, in the early stages of being an English major, I seldom wrote. I spent time at the coffee-house on campus where I chatted with other English majors and smoked Camel Lights and *talked about* writing. If I did manage to drink enough coffee to face my note-book, where I twitched and strained as I wrote a few incomprehensible pages, I seldom had the courage to look over what I had written. Indeed, being a literature major makes one a much stronger critic of literature than a producer of it.

In those caffeine-induced, raucous times at the coffeehouse, I began doing what I was meant to do, and that was tell tales, most of which pressed the limits of belief. Never in my wildest imagination, however, did I ever think that this was something worthy of anyone's time, let alone something that could become the focus of one's life.

An intermediary step—between being a writer and being one who tells stories out loud in front of audiences— was becoming a school teacher. In my classroom, I began publicly telling tales from my life and not simply for the benefit of one or two friends. "Secret Garden" is about how I became a teacher. The tale ends with my meeting my wife, moving back from Indonesia to the US, and then becoming a teacher.

This story also dramatizes a letting go of the romantic view of being a writer. In the tale, I wrote countless letters to a woman I had originally traveled to Indonesia to be with. These letters professed an undying love for a person that I didn't really know, let alone had trust and faith in. In many ways, the revelation that she left Indonesia without telling me represents the departure of this romantic attachment to writing for the sake of writing.

The story ends with my writing letters to someone that I really did develop a deep love for. Instead of writing descriptions of physical beauty and fantastic scenarios of lovemaking, the letters became reports of significant things that happened to me: getting married, becoming a teacher, having children—the very things that I tell stories about.

TELLING TALES IN EARNEST

*A*fter a great deal of psychological analysis and introspection, I have come to the conclusion that I became a storyteller to fill a terrible and oppressive silence that haunts me. Into that silence, I stammer and stutter, frenetically searching for connections of loose ends... some point of stability upon which to rest. The people in my life became characters... Boobie Eisterholtz, Corky Tilton, Konsuma, my father-in-law, my wife, and my own children. They became flattened stock types in that they behaved according to a set of rules. But at the same time, their behaviors, though following a simple logic, led to actions that were fired in the deepest, most desperate reaches of my imagination.

I was afraid of silence at my family dinner table, for in that silence, I sensed disapproval from my own mother. I created most of this myself, I believe, but there were many occasions when my childhood friends sensed her general disapproval. This included all of my girlfriends, and even my wife to this very day.

I suppose my mother inspired my primal, mythical impulse to speak. We are all prompted by our mothers when we are tossed in their arms, nuzzled, and showered with nonsensical sounds, but perhaps mine was a touch less vocal, or perhaps I was a touch sensitive to her stare, which I thought seemed hardened and unsatisfied.

As a child in early elementary school, I think I probably could have shut down and not spoken, or I could have spoken abundantly, without really any point, which is what I did. I would report the activities of the day, and from an early age, my task was to keep a smile on the faces of my mother and father. At times, this required stretching the truth. I believe we are born with a sense of how a story should go.

My earliest stories were about classmates, and the intent of my stories is now painfully clear. I told my parents at the dinner table about a fellow first-grader, Joseph, who misbehaved. He was out of his chair; he let the classroom pet, a mouse, loose; when told to go to the office he marched like a soldier, "Hut, two, three, four..." All of this was true, but I could already feel the urge to elaborate so that my mother and father would be pleased with me, who was passing myself off as a passive, objective, well-behaved observer. A story is crafted by the needs of the audience.

On a day when Joseph had done nothing out of the ordinary, my father asked, "Well, what did he do today?" I quietly indicated that not much had happened, and my father shrugged and went on eating his slice of canned ham.

"Nothing?" my mother demanded. "I don't see how anyone can possibly put up with him." She stabbed at her green beans. Silence set in. My brother was miserably pushing his food from one side of the plate to the other. My mother dropped her fork and knife and glared at one of us and then the other. She studied my brother, who scooped his army-green-hued beans along with a band of ham fat into his napkin and then swept it into his lap. My father ate the small piece of ham skewered on his fork like he smoked a cigarette. He took a small bite, and then twirled the fork dexterously between his fingers, like he was deeply contemplating some engineering problem from the office.

Was it me? I could feel pressure building, like something was going to explode. I'm pretty sure the source of the explosion would be my mother. She had, in fact, exploded before. I don't know what started it, but once I remember her shouting over and over again that we were lucky we had a mother like her. "Lucky!" she shouted. "Lucky!" Her round glasses made her look like a fierce predatory bird.

"Actually, I just remembered... Joseph did do something."

"Oh?" my father said, and then plucked the ham off the fork with his lips. He lit a cigarette. My mother turned her head in my direction. My brother happily swept the entire ham cutlet like a Frisbee off his plate into the living room. I began.

"We had poetry presentations. Joseph's was about love. He had chosen it on purpose because it mentioned the lips of a lover over and over. Each time he mentioned lips, he would curl his like the foot of a snail. 'Your lips…' he would say, and look right at Mrs. Johnson."

"Is that all?" my mother demanded.

"No," I said. "There's more. He pulled from his pocket a red marker and began to color his lips."

"What was the class doing?" Dad asked, chuckling.

"They were trying not to laugh," I said.

"What were *you* doing?" my mother demanded.

I continued the story. "He made his lips into thick red clown lips and then began to make kissing noises. He was making gross sounds like 'Oh, yeah… Oh…' Then more kissing noises."

"What about the teacher?" My mother pounded the table with her fist, making my father jump.

"She was angry," I said. "Really angry. She took Joseph by the shoulders and he began to march—'Hut, two, three, four'—all the way to the door. She told him he had to go wash his face. He went, but not before he asked her if she liked his big red lips. 'No I don't,' she stammered. 'I think you do,' he said, and then left."

"That Joseph," my father quipped.

"Is that all your teacher did? I would have suspended him," my mother announced. She leaned towards my brother and me. "If *you guys* ever do anything like *that*, I am going to *paddle* you so you never forget it." There was silence. She looked at us both. My father sighed. "Do you understand?" she demanded even more loudly.

The correct answer was "yes," I suppose, but nobody did understand. Nobody ever understood why she was so unhappy with us.

"*Do you understand?*" she shouted.

"I'm not finished," I said. I swear my father gave a sigh of relief.

"It was Sarah Lynch's turn to say her poem," I began. "Hers was about a flounder. It had a big, dead eye. Mrs. Johnson really liked the poem, and you could hear her making noises while Sarah was speaking like 'Good, Sarah. Oh, Sarah. Wow!'"

"What was your poem?" my mother interrupted aggressively, but that didn't stop me. I suddenly knew what happened. "Sarah didn't finish her poem because Joseph came back in the room."

"What? I thought he got kicked out," my mother said.

"Dripping wet," I said with relish. "He tried to wash off the red pen, but it smeared even more and now he looked like the Joker! His shirt was wet—so were his pants. His shoes made squishing noises."

"Why was he so wet?" my mother demanded. She hadn't followed that he had been sent to wash off the red pen.

"He marched right up to where Mrs. Johnson was sitting at her desk. *Squish! Squish! Squish!*"

I had them. Everyone. Even my brother, who was unloading the mashed potatoes from his plate (he had a sack of Halloween candy he was living on) was looking straight at me, his fork between his plate and the serving bowl.

"Then Joseph smashed his face right into Mrs. Johnson's!" I said. It was the climax.

"Was he biting her?" my mother shrieked.

"No," I said. "Worse. He was kissing her and making those noises—kissing noises, like 'Oh... Mmm... Oh...'"

There was silence, but it was a more comfortable

silence; all of the tension had been drained out of the room.

"He was sent home," I said matter-of-factly. Then, the dénouement: "Mrs. Johnson had to leave class because she had red pen all over her white blouse."

I took a bite of ham and then casually added—in case my mother still hadn't gotten it—"From all the kissing Joseph did on her shirt."

I never had to say what my poem was about. It hadn't meant anything to me. It had simply seemed like poetry to me. It was a short one. I remember it was about death. I also remember there was a line about maggots in it.

It was true that Joseph acted out in class. He'd marched, "Hut, two, three, four." He'd mentioned lips in class in an obsessive way once. We were diagramming a fish. Mrs. Johnson had stated, "Fish have lips." She wrote *lips* on the overhead projector and drew a line to the fish's mouth.

"Lips," Joseph repeated loudly.

She shushed him, and then repeated, "Fish have lips."

Joseph said again, very loudly, "I know fish have lips."

And so it had gone. He was marched to the office. He was eventually taken out of our class. Before this, I remember, he had a cast on his arm. The true story of Joseph was probably very tragic. I never included the detail that he smelled really bad: like unwashed clothes and sometimes like feces.

On the day of the poetry recitation, he had not recited a poem at all. The part about kissing and the lips had sprung from my third grade imagination, in an attempt to distract my family from my mother's mysterious dissatisfaction.

I never made her happy with my stories, I realize. At

best, I simply forestalled her inevitable tirades. So, my first audience was not a healthy, balanced one. It was one that had to be grappled with and overpowered. It was one that was quick to jump in whenever there were any inconsistencies, and even when there weren't. I was telling stories, at times, it seemed, to save my very life. This led to a great deal of anxiety, and it still does today when I get up to perform.

THE PERFORMER'S ANXIETY ON THE STAGE

"The ambulance driver told me there was not really anything to do for a scorpion bite, and—in case I hadn't noticed—he was kind of busy."

My mind went completely blank. I had no idea what the next line was. I stepped back from the microphone. I caught a glimpse of my friend smiling from his seat at the bar. His smile faded. He knew I had blanked out. The entire audience knew.

I recovered and finished, but there had been no hiding the fact that I had blanked out for a few seconds. What's worse was this performance at the open mic was supposed to bolster my confidence for the Moth StorySLAM at the Berkeley Freight & Salvage Coffeehouse. Instead, the experience had shattered it.

On the drive home, I put a bandage on the open, bleeding part of the story where I had forgotten what came next. I added a physical gesture right where I had blanked out. Of course, there were a thousand other places in that story that could burst open and gush all over the stage in front of everyone. While that part of the story was tightened, it had done little to dispel my anxiety.

I had high levels of anxiety even when going to nursery school. This morphed into test anxiety in elementary school and middle school. By high school, I was getting up at three in the morning to "over-prepare" for even the smallest of tests or quizzes. Eventually, I started memorizing large sections of textbooks, including entire short stories in French. This was a pattern that would plague me through college, and it has reared its head again as I struggle with performance anxiety. Even now, to feel more in control on stage, just as that nervous, misguided teen did preparing for exams, I memorize my stories.

I distinctly remember how this started. My mother had once been a middle school French teacher, but was forced into early retirement when public schools began to drop foreign language from the curriculum. She took it upon herself to teach me French during elementary school and middle school. She was proud that I tested out of basic French and went directly into second year.

This meant I had class with my neighbor, Maki. She was a year older than me, and although we lived next to each other, starting around the fourth or fifth grade, I saw her from afar, surrounded by boys that I wouldn't dare talk to. In middle school, I was walking home and passed her as she lounged on the rail of a bridge over a creek. She was with other girls, wearing bell bottom jeans and smoking. We pretended not to know one another, and frankly, we didn't. Our years of playing in my yard or hers were gone.

Once we had "run away" from home together and lived on her back deck for a week, purchasing food from her father for pennies.

Out of the blue, Maki phoned during my freshman year. Her voice was cheery, like the musical notes of laughter at a party. I looked out the kitchen window and saw her, like I had seen so many times, as she held the phone, standing in her kitchen. I held my hand up hesitantly, and she waved back. She wanted me to come over to study French. When I arrived with my book, her family cheered—help had arrived. We went downstairs to her bedroom.

Through her bedroom window, I looked back at my own house, my mother walking to and fro in the kitchen, the blurred shape of my brother watching television in the downstairs family room. My own bedroom window was dark. I wondered if Maki noticed how early my bedroom light went on in the morning as I made my obsessive, unnecessary reviews.

I had been in her room many times before, but years earlier. There were toys then, and for some reason, a large set of *National Geographic* magazines. I looked at them with her. Once, she tossed one in front of me and told me it was the War. On the cover was a mother holding a child. Looking back, I realize it was the cover of an issue about Vietnam. The baby's leg had deep, pink—but bloodless —wounds.

"How come they don't look sad?" I asked.

She picked up the magazine. "I think they look sad."

Now, her room was different. The smell of fresh

laundry and parental attention had given way to the private space of a sixteen-year-old girl. I glanced around at the boxes of rings and earrings. Hanging from little hooks along the top of her mirror were necklaces. The room smelled strongly of perfume; or rather, perfumes—a mixture—some sweet like candy and others loaded with citrus.

Lotions and creams lined the window sill. The window faced my house, and later from my home when I looked back at her room, I would be able to pick out the jar she suddenly grabbed and spun open. She dipped her straightened index and middle finger deep into the cream and scraped out a dollop the way I would with cake batter from a mixing bowl. A smell that made me think of white flowers in the night overpowered the candy and citrus smells, and I felt a twinge of anxiousness—just like I used to get when my second grade teacher approached my desk, her perfume announcing her presence.

Maki pulled a chair from in front of the mirror and moved it next to her unmade bed. Her sheets and blankets seemed impossibly twisted together. She apologized for how messy her room was. I sat in the chair, my knees pressed against her bed, as she crawled alongside me, almost encircling me. Up close, I could see blue particles beneath her eyes—she wore makeup.

She kept the dictionary next to her, and I could see her neat large writing scrawled over the French text we were reading—*aperture, evangelism, docket*—other words she searched in her *Petit Larousse*. We had to be ready for anything. *What was on the table when the woman entered?*

What was the man's scar like? What was his beard like? I rushed into the details of the story, my mind flying in a thousand directions as to what the possible questions would be.

Two hours went by, and it was ten o'clock and time for me to go. I was going to get up at three the next morning. She remained on her bed as I left, and there was always a softness that came over her eyes. At the time, I remember feeling a shiver up my spine, never having gotten any attention from a young woman my age. I realize now it was pity—pity for how exhausted she imagined I must be and how pointless it was that I was hurling this much energy into an insignificant French quiz. One night, before I left, she told me I didn't need to get up in the morning. "You practically have the entire story memorized," she said.

I never failed to notice this softness in her. I marked its growth over the course of evenings spent with her, hunched over our book of French short stories. Her eyes were like river stones that would slowly grow darker and shinier with the trickle of something from within gently and slowly moistening them. I found my beautiful neighbor sprawled on a bed in front of me to be totally disarming.

The last time I studied French with Maki, I had memorized a significant amount of Guy de Maupassant's "The Necklace." I was spewing the beginning paragraphs at her while she fumbled along, stopping me to ask what a word meant, and then writing it in the margin of her book. I was enjoying the awed look on Maki's face as I blasted through the story, but I was also feeling a great deal of comfort that

I was perfectly prepared for Monsieur Peterson's worst. To do this, I had copied every sentence of the story over and over. Was it to prepare for the test, or was it to impress my beautiful neighbor? In answer to this, I would say that consciously it was for the French test, but subconsciously, it had been for her.

As I launched into a description of the protagonist, Mathilde, on the one night of extravagance she was ever to enjoy in her life, a beautiful necklace adorning her white throat, I didn't notice that Maki had leaned back in her bed and thrown an arm behind her head. She propped herself up with her pillow and stared as I ripped through the paragraphs, trying to assure myself that my knowledge of the story was solid.

I held the book shut, concentrating on the solid red cover, trusting that she would stop and correct me if I missed anything in my recitation, but she was no longer following along. When Mathilde's hand suddenly shot to her throat to find it bare of the necklace she had borrowed from her rich friend, I briefly glanced up to observe Maki as she arched her back on the bed and looked at her thumb and index finger, which she rubbed together. I paused, and then I stumbled on the next line describing how Mathilde's chest rose and fell, her face flushing. Maki noticed that I stopped. For a moment, we locked eyes.

"I lost where we are," she said, flipping the pages aimlessly.

I became lightheaded. A feeling came over me—one that has since become all too familiar—that everything around me wasn't real. My heart pounded, and I couldn't think of the title of the story we were reading, let alone the page we were on.

Maki rescued me. "It's somewhere around page 96," she said, and then pulled a twisted bedsheet across herself.

"Right," I said, reading a line and then tossing the book aside as I launched back into a recitation of the story.

On the way home, all I thought about was whether or not I would be able to recall the story when I was taking the test. The next morning I got up at three to go over it, again and again.

The next time we had an upcoming French test, I stared through the trees that separated our houses. I could see her in the kitchen with her family. She didn't phone, and deep disappointment and hurt welled up from my seldom-examined feelings. What I thought was simply an intense dread of our French test was probably my first heartache. Of course, now it is clear how little I had helped her French, and how those displays in which I had recited entire paragraphs of the story and was completely inattentive to her, if anything, had only made her more anxious about the test.

I am certain that Maki was thinking about other, older boys. This was made evident when a Volkswagen Beetle with a surfboard attached to the roof began parking in her family's driveway around the same time as the last study session. An opportunity had been missed. In addition to being neighbors, there had been potential to be friends, but my desperate spewing of words had eliminated this possibility.

At that point in my life, I was still performing at the dinner table for the benefit of my mother. Her long silences and severe expressions would often prompt one of us to ask her if anything was wrong. It was during these heavy silences that I would improvise. Just as middle school had, high school brought a new cast of characters. One in particular captured the fancy of my family: Randy T.

"What kind of last name is T.?" my mother shouted, making my father jump as he swiped a pineapple from the canned ham we seemed to always be eating.

I had no idea. I wasn't making him up. That was what was on the attendance roster. That was how he wrote his name on his assignments. Randy T. was real, and somewhat of an exhibitionist. This would lead to his constant hovering around the open mic that was set up on the front lawn every lunchtime. Randy T. would take the microphone and begin to taunt people—his go-to insult would simply reference everyone's mother.

"Your mother!" he would shout and point at someone. "And yours too!"

Eventually our dean, who wandered around campus during lunch and break with a hockey stick, slowly approached and shooed Randy T. away from the microphone with a gentle but steady sweeping motion of his stick.

"Why is he always yelling about people's mothers?" my own mother demanded.

"He's taunting people," I said. "Because somebody's mother is the most important thing they have." This seemed to appease her.

On an evening when my mother was particularly surly, I recall spinning quite an elaborate yarn. Randy T. had been shouting about people's mothers again in what I had slowly developed into a very loud voice with a Boston accent.

"Ya mutha! And yo-was!"

The dean approached with his stick, but this time, something different happened. Before Randy T. exited, he took the microphone with him. "It was wireless," I said anticipating an interruption from my mother.

She changed her tack. "Why did he want the microphone?"

I held my hand up as if to say, *I'm getting there.*

I continued. "The dean followed Randy T. into the bushes behind the lawn. You could see the hockey stick moving like a shark fin as the dean slowly made his way in ever-tightening circles through the brush.

"Meanwhile, the student council set up the regular microphone, the one with a cord, and they were announcing the upcoming walk-a-thon. The president was in the middle of saying something about whom the fundraiser would benefit when loud and clear, presumably from the bushes, Randy T., with his wireless mic, overrode the sound system. "Ya muthas!"

The president halted. "No, it will benefit those with multiple sclerosis," he corrected.

"Just like ya mutha!" Randy T. boomed from the bushes.

My father's shoulders were silently shaking with laughter.

"You think this is funny?" my mother challenged my father. "I think he is a smarty pants!" This was my mother's term reserved for those she most strongly disapproved of.

"Ya mutha!" my brother, who was in middle school,

repeated. I thought I was succeeding in transforming the dismal canned ham atmosphere, but then I realized I was wrong.

Slam! My mother's fist hit the table. "I don't think I want to hear anymore about Randy T.!" she bellowed, and then turned the tables on us. "If I ever hear of you guys doing anything like this…"

"You won't hear any more about Randy T.," I said. "He's gone"—I paused dramatically and then added with a very serious tone—"probably forever."

Everyone stared at me.

"Well," my mother stammered sheepishly. "What happened?"

I launched back into the story.

"Suddenly there was shouting and grunting over the sound system. The president had to stop the walk-a-thon announcement, and everyone on the front lawn turned towards the bushes. Like the outlaw that he was, Randy T. busted out of the bushes with the dean just a hockey stick length behind him and sprinted through everyone, right past the president, who had to step out of the way."

"Where was he going?" my mother shrieked.

"Nobody knew. The last thing he did was stop in the parking circle behind the small stage area. He turned and shouted into the wireless microphone that was still in his hand, 'You're all a buncha muthas!' Then he dropped the mic right on the asphalt. The dean, his hockey stick dangling at his side, stood and watched Randy T. run right down Miller Avenue.

"He still hasn't returned," I finished dramatically.

~

My first audiences were individual women. While I was hyper-aware of my fearsome mother, I had been totally oblivious to the seductive Maki. Whereas I improvised and spun yarns to appease the volatile beast that lurked within my mother, in the five times I sat in front of Maki as she reclined on her bed, I had resorted to filling the awkward silences with the lines from the story that I had memorized.

I had found the prospect of silence in either situation, both the disapproval and scorn from my mother or a fear of rejection by a beautiful girl that was so repressed that I wasn't even conscious of it, to be something to be avoided at all costs. Because of these transformative experiences, I have become hard-wired to fill silence with story, to hurl words sacrificially into a pit where there lies a hungry, angry, disarming, and beautiful goddess.

And now, in my fifties, as I stand in front of the microphone and the audience falls silent, I am right back at my kitchen table, trembling in front of the inexhaustible and incomprehensible—my mother's unhappiness. With time, I lost the confidence to improvise, which I had been able to do in her familiar albeit frightening presence. I have resorted to finding safety in memorizing my stories, as I did for Maki.

Halfway through my freshman year, someone new joined our second year French class. My best friend's cousin Kim moved to the Bay Area from Florida and started attending our high school. She, too, was a fresh-man, and in her, I found not only someone my own age but also someone who worried just as much as I did about grades. She fretted to the point of extreme action. In response to the detailed and somewhat nit-picky questions, she too memorized entire short stories in French. She too had been placed in biology, and she too copied over chapters from the biology book.

Prior to tests, we began meeting at break or lunch and reciting passages we had committed to memory—whether about the flow of energy through the ecosystem or what Monsieur Lebiou's pipe looked and smelled like. Some days we would switch between the condescending English prose of a high school textbook to the flowery, literary French of whatever Monsieur Peterson was having us read —Maupassant, Flaubert, Mérimée...

Rather than showing concern about this behavior, teachers praised us for it, even rewarded it. And we began to sit next to one another at the front of the class, causing the sophomores to roll their eyes. I once heard Maki, who sat in the back of the class, tell other students that we were perfect for each other, and belonged together—studying. Indeed, we phoned each other every night, and would fall into a rhythm chanting French prose or listing things from the biology book. But finally, at a dance, we kissed.

In an obvious way, our friends walked us to a deserted bench and then very deliberately left us together. We allowed ourselves to be trapped, and ignored the laughter of our friends as they walked away. Naturally, we immediately fell into a recitation of Maupassant's "The Necklace."

Without any thought as to the meaning of the story, and how ironically, the loss of the necklace makes Mathilde a hard-working, honest person after her having previously lived a superficial life, we blasted through passages about her washing floors, shopping in the public market, scouring dishes, and mending the shreds of clothing she and her husband were forced to wear, all because she had lost her rich friend's necklace.

Our recitation captured none of the drama, either; it was purely a demonstration of knowledge of the text's details: Mathilde's hands became shiny and red from labor; her hair was tied simply and practically; she shouted gossip from her knees while swiping wide swaths across the floor.

As we chanted the text, our foreheads drew together. The side of Kim's long leg pressed against mine, and the downy hair of her temples brushed my cheek. We were reaching the dramatic twist of the story—the moment when Mathilde meets her wealthy friend whose necklace she has lost and has taken on a lifetime of debt to replace. I could feel puffs of breath from Kim's mouth as she picked up the pace, racing to the end, when the rich friend reveals that the necklace she has borrowed is fake; not worth anything. Kim shivered. Our cheeks touched, and before we could take the last line to its conclusion, we rolled our faces along each other's and pressed our lips together.

She opened her mouth wide, which surprised me. My mouth, which was closed, actually slipped inside hers, only stopped from going to the very back of her throat by the barriers of her upper and lower teeth, which caught and held my chin and philtrum. We pushed our faces together, our hands dangling uselessly in our laps. That was how we stayed for what seemed like fifteen minutes. Neither one of us dared to pull back, because that would have meant looking at one another.

In spite of the uncomfortable sensation my lips were experiencing against her incisors, I held ground with my lips inside her mouth. Once or twice I opened my eyes only to see the tiny, delicate veins that laced within her thin eyelids, which she held loosely shut, like she was enjoying a peaceful sleep. Though I wasn't moving my mouth, I could taste something like postage stamps. What I wasn't aware of was that a large loop of drool had begun to hang beneath us, having first collected on the delicate bulb of her chin. We were eventually saved from the kiss by our friends, who returned to cheer and tease. Kim sprang up and ran to the safety of the other girls, holding her arms straight as if they held the tension of her embarrassment. I wiped my mouth and chin with my sleeve. To my horror, the leg of my pants was soaked with drool; I attempted to wipe that off as well.

We never kissed again. Our time was spent together strictly reciting French passages, whether in person in our high school's hallways or over the phone.

My family life went the way of my love life, and I resorted to reciting French short stories at the dinner table. As my father sliced the ham, and as my brother shoveled things under the seat cushion, I would compulsively hold forth, speaking rapid, polished French, waving chunks of ham skewered on my fork to emphasize certain passages. I stopped only to flip through the book, which I kept in my lap to check a line or two or to allow my mother to correct my pronunciation. In so doing, while pacifying my mother, I think I temporarily killed the storyteller inside of me, one that had protected me from my mother's wrath, one that I had sent forth to win the love of young women.

During my senior year, in a way that is typical of teenagers, I fell silent, and I let my family be the dysfunctional, uncomfortable mess that I had always known it was.

THE AUDIENCE IS NOT MY MOTHER

For years, the storyteller lay dead at the bottom of my soul, coming out of hiding briefly in the college coffeehouse, only to be sent back into hiding—until I became a teacher. Fate had it that I was to become a teacher of students who were the very same age as I had been when I shut off the creative storyteller—ninth grade. Perhaps I was drawn to this age because it was such a significant year in my life. It was probably no coincidence that I began to resurrect the missing part of myself.

I had to let go of wanting to be a professor first of chemistry and then of English. Perhaps most importantly, I had to let go of aiming to write the Great American Novel. Maybe more than any other year, the ninth grade had sent me on this path away from storytelling, and I had returned to recover something of it, and it happened unintentionally.

I wanted my students to enjoy humanities class and to not be steeped in anxiety as I had been. Therefore, I wanted to give them something as far from my experience as a ninth grader as I could. I wanted to connect with them about the material I taught, not wield it over them as Monsieur Peterson and all the others in my education had.

I was particularly sympathetic to the students who seemed nervous and anxious. Every year, I seem to get more and more of these. I wanted to heal these young people who suffered from short attention spans and panic disorders, as if that would somehow eliminate the years of anxiety and worry over grades I had suffered. I began to do this with stories.

I told stories about my years in Indonesia. Since it was an independent school, I was allowed to teach a long, detailed unit on Indonesian history and literature. I began to weave stories of the Gasconade River, where I'd spent joyful summers imagining myself to be like Tom Sawyer and Huck Finn, into discussions of the Ancient river valleys. I learned Indian, African, Chinese, Tibetan, Korean, and of course, Indonesian folktales to bring the study of these places to life. For twelve happy years, my ninth graders were my audience, and the classroom was my story lab.

Of course, I told stories about my family. Many of the stories I told to these ninth graders dramatized my relationship with my mother. Over the years I perfected an abrasive, aggressive, and demanding tone that was so horrific that my students burst into laughter every time I employed it. "Is that what your mother sounds like?" they asked, and I inevitably told them in reality she was much worse.

While I confess it makes one wonder how some of this fit into a humanities curriculum, I told a long epic about the ham dinners our family suffered, the canned ham hissing and ticking on the table like a bomb. My family dinner table scenarios were filled with despair over eating ham every night for ten years, my father's attempts to smooth things over so he could have just a few moments of peace after a long day of work, and the impetuous outbursts from my mother when she shouted, accused, and slammed things around. I took the ham dinners to the next level by introducing my Jewish best friend who didn't eat ham.

"Uh oh," the class chimed, knowing that an explosion from my mother was imminent.

"My father scraped the burnt, greasy pineapples onto his plate and told him to eat those," I said. The next week I introduced a vegetarian, death-rocker girlfriend into the dinner scenarios.

I only ran into problems with performance anxiety when I began to tell these stories on stage, especially in at story slams and contests, in which storytellers are scored against one another. For these, I had to polish my tales and time them. My audience was no longer the ninth-grade version of myself. I was no longer telling the stories to nurture and heal, but, once again as I had with my mother, to impress. This is when I began obsessively rehearsing, just as I had during the years of French and biology.

Early on in my career outside the classroom, I performed at the Throckmorton Theatre, in Mill Valley where my parents still live. To my horror, my parents found out about the performance and announced they would be attending. I couldn't stop thinking about the rows of tables, the seats in the balcony, the stage lights beaming right on me; and right there, at the foot of the stage at a table in the front, would be my mother.

To make matters worse, I had been asked to tell a particular story, one that featured my mother—in full abrasive voice, tyrannical judgment, and all. In the days leading up to the performance, I worried about having my script memorized, but I vacillated between that and the fear of the look on my mother's face if I went through with my impersonation of her. I honestly thought this would be it—the time my knees really would buckle on the stage, the time my mind really would go completely blank in front of three hundred people.

I barely remember being on stage, and because the stage lights were so bright, I couldn't see my mother. I got to the part of the story where I imitated my mother's voice. I paused. I could still make her sound respectful, caring, and nurturing. It wasn't too late. But that wasn't the real story.

I could see a couple sitting to the right and a group of young men on the left in the front row. Right in the middle, not much more than an arm's length away, lost in the soup of purple, blue, and gold light was my mother. I could sense her.

The theater fell completely silent, and some in the audience might have thought I forgot my next line. Little did they know what kind of predicament I faced, or what kind of debate raged in my head. The silence continued, and in this silence was perhaps the only power greater than any concern I had for myself or my relationship with my family. I had to tell the story, and her voice in the story made her sound like a monster.

I did it. I belted out her demanding, horrible, tyrannical voice with everything I had. From the corner of my eye, I could see the couple convulsing violently with laughter. The young men cheered. It was going over well. As I cast myself further and further into the audience's embrace, I was aware I was also digging myself deeper and deeper into a hole—one that I knew I could never again climb out of. This is what a final show felt like—my swan song.

I remained petrified to the end of the show. At that point, I had to go into the lobby for the inevitable meeting with my wife and parents. But, as I approached, they didn't seem disturbed. In fact, even though I had seen them recently, they just looked old, stooped and somewhat weathered. They were gently smiling as they greeted all the other neighbors and friends who had attended.

My father saw me and clapped his hand on my shoulder. "You were the best one," he said cheerily.

My mother chimed in. "That was really good."

I was stunned.

As I stood there in disbelief, a woman approached us and asked, "Now, that isn't really what your mother sounds like, is it?"

My father intervened. "Good God! That's his mother right there! Does she look capable of sounding like that?" He laughed. "No, no. He just makes all this stuff up."

The woman looked a little disappointed. "You mean none of it is true?"

My mother added, "He used to tell us these ridiculous stories at the dinner table. They were absolutely outrageous, and there was no way any of it could have happened." She turned to me. "Who was it you used to always go on about? Randy T.?"

"Ah," my father said, clapping me on the shoulder. "I remember Old Randy T.! He's the guy that kept stealing the microphone!"

"He was real!" I stated, more to the woman than to my parents. "And he did most of those things. And the story I just told *was* true." I began to stammer. "Except for how my mother sounds."

I listened to myself as I defended the details, and to my frustration, it only seemed to amuse my parents. I hadn't spoken to them recently about the stories I'd told them at the dinner table—about Joseph, Randy T. and all the other characters that were featured: Kennel, Waffle, Jordan, Monsieur Peterson, F. Bob, and Lighty—but I was surprised that they remembered any of the details about Randy T. I was arrested by the fact that they had never believed any of it. What was most perplexing about this was that they had never taken these stories seriously. I recalled being very serious and earnest as I was telling them.

"That was true," I insisted once again, but my mother blurted, "Oh, it was not!"

But what was true? I had to ask myself this question. Why was it so important to me that my parents and everyone else believe my story was true? Randy T. was real. He really did stand in front of the microphone more than anyone should have, but he never sprinted into the parking lot, and he definitely did not disappear. He was there to take the microphone from its stand the next day and the next. He ended up in the part of the school that is devoted to students with behavioral problems, but he graduated alongside me.

The truth of the story lay beneath the surface, and not in the details. It lay in the earnestness and sincerity with which I told it to my parents. At the time of the telling, I recall feeling that my parents', especially my mother's, love for me was in jeopardy. This was enough to produce a level of intense conviction rivaled only by my concern for the grades that I got in school.This is why I find myself so often compulsively weaving yarns for those in my life, especially the women, as if my very life depended upon holding their attention and making them smile at all costs.

The disparity between how I perceived the past and how my parents recollected it has become an important question for me. It aligns with how I perceive my audience as being the same unhappy, tyrannical, monster that I made my mother out to be. I believe there was always a seed of unhappiness in her, but in the same way that Joseph and Randy T. were transformed into characters, I also invented a version of my mother. That version now adorns many of the tales I tell, especially to my ninth graders.

Realizing that she is a character in a tale may have been the important first step in overcoming my anxiety on stage. If I have freed my mother from the version of her in my tales so that I can love her for who she is, then maybe I can begin to approach my audience with love rather than fear.

TAKING STORYTELLING SERIOUSLY

*a*side from my father shaking with silent laughter from time to time, I never remember my parents enjoying my dinner table stories. The stories were told to hold their attention and forestall their anger. Along with learning they'd never believed any of it, the fact that they were amused by them was another revelation. It was another step towards seeing my parents for who they are, and also towards seeing the audience realistically. I have learned to reimagine the audience as capable of being amused and entertained, not simply as a group sitting back and judging me harshly.

Since my performance at the Throckmorton Theatre, my parents have come to several other shows, and expressed their wholehearted enjoyment. Of course, I am relieved that they do not take any of my caricatures seriously. But that doesn't mean that the stories shouldn't be taken seriously.

A tale can be amusing and entertaining, but I have learned that in every tale that is told, there is a very serious desire to connect with the audience. The flow of discourse may be in one direction, but there is a powerful flow of energy back to the teller. It is coded and telegraphed through gesture, posture, facial expression, gasps, applause, shock, silence, and so many of the more subtle and nuanced forms of communication.

I suppose I was always—more than anything else— trying to connect with my family. Over the past few years, I have also been trying to connect with audiences. My way of connecting is by telling stories. Maybe that is the best answer I will ever get to the question as to why I am compelled to tell stories. It is exhilarating to feel that I did a good job on the stage, but it is a deeper, richer feeling of happiness to speak with members of the audience who shake my hand and don't let go as they tell me a story of their own.

There are many other ways a person can connect with another, and there are some people who will never resort to formal storytelling. But there are times when standing on a stage in front of a live audience is the best way. The third chapter of this volume, "Telling Stories Around the Fire," is a survey of tales told at an event to commemorate the Tubbs Fire of October 9, 2017. I was honored to be the host for an evening of stories told by first responders and victims.

I was not a victim of these fires, so there were many times that I felt like an absolute imposter as the host of this event. However, I had already learned the power of stories to create a connection between storytellers and their audiences. This was what I focused on as I curated the event and worked with the storytellers through very disturbing and traumatic material.

"Why would anyone want to relive all of that?" someone quipped when I told them about my project. I think this person was imagining what many were: that it would be a night of dismal sadness and re-lived trauma.

It turns out it couldn't have been further from the truth. The power of turning experiences into formal stories for the stage broke up what were simply unmanageable amounts of raw trauma into moments that were funny and hopeful as well as tragic and crushing. There were moments that served as a build-up in relation to moments that were significant climaxes, moments that were hopeful dénouements as well as ones where the teller burst into tears.

Beneath these stories was not the hurt of the teller or the outrage that this happened to them and not to others, but that same desire to connect to others—those that were victims and those that weren't. This is the true magic of storytelling.

When the audience members first arrived at the theater, they were in different places in relation to the fire. Some had lost everything, while others hadn't been affected. Some had volunteered tirelessly at shelters or had fought the fires as first responders, while others had hunkered down in their homes to listen to the news on KSRO radio. And then, in the indifferent march of time after the fires, many had moved on, forgetting those who still had not found permanent places to live or those who still grieved for family lost in the flames.

On that night, as we listened to the tales unfold, we

were all connected in the same place at the same time. Those who hadn't lost anything were right there with those who had lost everything. Those that had lost everything were reassured by their power to move a large audience and bring us all back to the night of the fires.

The evening of stories taught me the most important lesson about live storytelling. A tale is an invitation. It is like an extended hand. It is a gesture made by the teller— not to impress or simply entertain, though that can be an important part of it—but also to know the listener in one of the deepest and most human of ways.

Privately with a friend or family member, we hold hands when we aim to comfort them in times of sadness, but also to celebrate with them over an accomplishment. A simple gesture can hold many different meanings, but at the same time, it always conveys that you are there for the person and that you are listening. When storytellers take the stage, making themselves totally vulnerable, they are extending a hand to you and inviting you to laugh with them, or cry with them, but more than anything, to stop the passage of time for a moment and be together.

As you read this volume, I am not there in person to connect with you the way I might at a live storytelling event. The videos for the three tales contained in this volume are to be found at brandonspars.com. There are also videos for many other performances I have done in the past few years there.

However, watching a video, even though it features the voices and sound effects I use while telling, still isn't the same as watching a live performance. Hopefully one of the values of this book is that in reading the tales or watching the videos, you will be inspired to go to a live storytelling event, maybe even one with me in it. If you do, remember what a risk the storyteller is taking by standing on the stage; and, most importantly, remember to do your part as an audience member, which is to focus every fiber in your body on connecting.

PART II
THE STORIES

A BIG NIGHT OUT

I was at a crossroads in my life—a real crisis. I was a chemistry major in college, but I was miserable. It was the summer between my junior and senior year, and I was staying at my parents' house on a river in the state of Missouri, where my mother is from. That was when I read a book called *Siddhartha* by Hermann Hesse, and in this book the protagonist finds focus and direction for his life. He may have even become enlightened. I am still not quite sure what happened to him at the end of the book. But the way he achieved it! He ended up living on a river, and speaking to the river, and hearing its responses. Now, I had always loved my river in Missouri, and I think deep down inside I thought that this river could talk to me. So, for the next several days, I sat and I stared at the river for hours, and I heard nothing.

I felt I had to get closer. I needed to go to the source of the river. I needed to spend hours gliding along its surface, listening for the faintest whisper. I needed to spend nights sleeping on its banks. That was when I phoned up a friend of the family and had him drive me way upriver to the source. That was how I had my big night out—my big night out on the river.

This friend of the family was always telling stories about the river, and this was no exception. As he was driving, he asked, "You heard of a catfish?"

I said, "Yes."

He said, "You heard of a dogfish?"

I said, "No."

And then he proceeded in telling me how he had trained a fish to go and fetch his lure and bring it back. He didn't even need a rod with a line. He could throw the lure, and it would go and bring it back to him.

I interrupted him. I said, "Rich"—that's his name—"You know this river. You've lived on it all your life. Do you think you can talk to the river?"

He gave me a look, and he said, "Sure do."

"How do you know when it's talking to you? How do you know?"

He gave me a wink, and he said, "Brandon, you just know."

What I hadn't expected was how small the river was going to be at the source. Gliding along, listening for the faintest whisper? Ha! I had a rope slung over my shoulder and was dragging the canoe through what was essentially wet gravel. Every turn there'd be this log jam, and I'd have to unload the canoe, pitch it over the top, and reload it on the other side.

The worst thing was, in the hottest part of the day, around two o'clock, I think my mind was beginning to play tricks on me. As I was trudging through the wet gravel, I began to hear footsteps behind me. One time I was so sure I heard someone walking behind me, I threw the rope down, and I walked back upstream hollering, "Hello? Is somebody there? I can hear you!" Nobody.

That night, at my little campsite, I was exhausted. I was heartened by one thing. This big creek came in, doubling the size of the river, so I was hoping the next day I'd actually be able to paddle a little bit. I stared out at the water, that black glassy surface reflecting the luminescence of the night sky. For the first time that day, I did what I had come to do: I listened. "What is it saying, this river?"

CRUNCH. SPLASH. CRUNCH. SPLASH. *This time I was not imagining it.* Something was definitely walking downstream right into my campsite.

Sure enough, in the ring of light from my campfire an enormous shadow loomed, and a large man, with the biggest goddamn hat I have ever seen in my life, walked right into my campsite and sat opposite me at my fire. His hat hid his eyes, but I remember seeing his bright red lips, which stretched across his chin in a smile just like a river snake sunning itself on a rock.

"The name's Wino," he said, and he didn't say much else except that he came out into the woods from time to time "to dry out." I gathered he was some kind of a drinking man. But me? I began to bubble away nervously all about the book *Siddhartha* and how Siddhartha had become enlightened with the river by talking to it. I didn't want to be enlightened, but I wanted to talk to the river.

Then I made a connection I hadn't made before in my life. My grandmother used to pick me up at the airport and bring me to the house on the river, and she would always stop on the bridge and make me get out the first day I was there and say "Hello" to the river. And then a few weeks later when I left, she'd make me stand there on the bridge, and with tears in my eyes, I'd say, "Goodbye, river. Goodbye."

Without warning, Wino stood up and walked back out into the darkness, and I listened as those footsteps disappeared back upstream.

I began to think I probably sounded kind of strange. I might have even sounded a little crazy. Maybe I had even driven him out of my campsite. I resolved the next morning if he came by I'd invite him into my campsite and explain myself a little better. That was when I heard a snap and a crash, this time coming off the hill. Something big was moving down the hillside toward my campsite.

I walked over to the edge of the gravel bar where it met the woods. "Hello, Wino?" I called hopefully. "Is that you? I'm glad you're coming back. I need to explain myself a little bit."

This next sound made the hair on the back of my neck rise. The only way I can describe it was like a wolf howling through a garden hose. I backed up so close to the fire that I was *in* the fire, and in my hands I suddenly had the axe just as two glowing eyes appeared from those woods. They began to bounce up and down about a foot off the ground as whatever it was came charging at me. I brought the axe down on this thing, and it skidded through the gravel, and I saw hooves. It was a very angry, very small, wild pig. I don't know what I had done to make it so angry, but it circled around and came at me again. I don't know how many times I brought the axe down on that thing, how many times it charged me, but it was clear one of us was going to die that night. So I began to pitch everything from my campsite into the canoe, and I eventually just shoved off into the darkness, hitting every log and rock there was. I'll be danged if that angry little pig didn't launch itself and just start snorkeling right after me.

I paddled and paddled and paddled, and every time I thought I had gone far enough, I'd pull over, and I'd hear that angry squeal still echoing down the river valley. I don't know when it was. It was late, but I must have dozed off, and my canoe wedged on a rock on the bank.

Something woke me up. With a start, I sat bolt upright. A big leaf fell off my head. My cheek stung in the morning mist from where it had been resting on a bolt on the bottom of the canoe. I heard the knock of an oar. Out of the mist emerged a canoe, its passenger gliding effortlessly out in the swift current of the main channel.

"Wino!" I cheered.

He looked back at me with those unseen eyes beneath his hat.

"Last night I thought it was you, but it was a hog." Another leaf fell from my face.

Wino's lips were twisted into that same smile over his chin, just like that river snake on that rock. Without saying a word, he disappeared into the mist.

I had done nothing to reassure him that I wasn't mad as a hatter. I pulled over, and I made a cup of coffee, and I began to collect myself. Then I began to paddle. I think it became an unconscious goal for me to catch up to Wino and really explain myself, but every turn—nothing! I paddled and paddled all day, but I never saw him. I never saw him again.

Late that afternoon, I was done. I went into a farm-house and called up Rich and had him come pick me up.

Of course, on the ride home, he looked and me and asked, "Well, did you hear the voice of the river?"

"Oh," I moaned. "I was chased all night by a hog down the river."

He laughed and he laughed. It was the first time I had ever told him a story about the river. Then he began to tell me how I must have gone right through a stretch of river that is considered to be haunted. There had been a serial killer who killed seventy-three people and stuffed every one of the bodies in these deep holes in the water. I was about to tell him about Wino, but then I paused. We were driving across a bridge, and there was the river laid out beneath us, twinkling in the late afternoon light. In that pause, I think that's when I heard its first whisper. That silence between two stories told by two people who know the river and who love the river. I know Rich was hearing it too because he looked over at me and he gave me that same wink he'd given me before. In that silence between the stories was the voice of the river.

The river didn't speak in words. It was a gentle but steady urging, encouragement really, pure encouragement to never give up. When I returned that fall to school, I didn't sign up for chemistry classes. I ended up majoring in English literature. Because of that big night out on the river, I ended up becoming a humanities teacher. Because of that big night out, I think it all led to this night with me telling you a story.

Told at Coyote Tales
Kendall Jackson Wine Estate & Gardens
Santa Rosa, CA
September 17, 2017
For the video of this performance and others visit
brandonspars.com

SECRET GARDEN

*M*y college girlfriend was beautiful. She was 6'2", a runway model. I was sure I was in love. In reality, she just had me wrapped around her finger.

Going to bars or parties with her was a challenge. Men

would come at her from every direction. Once we went to a Billy Idol concert, and the Rebel Rocker himself selected her out of the thousands present and plucked her up on stage with him. I didn't see her until four and a half hours after the concert had ended. Car rides home on nights like this, I would be in a sullen mood, whereas her mood was completely brightened by the attention of other men; but she could completely defuse me by tumbling into my lap, tickling me, and insisting, "Nothing happened. You're not mad."

After we graduated from college, she decided to travel the world teaching English with a volunteer organization, so naturally I signed up, too. Whereas she received a glamorous post in the cosmopolitan city of Jakarta, I can't even show you on a map where they posted me—somewhere deep in the jungles of Sumatra where I was to teach English to a recently-settled nomadic forest group.

After I said goodbye to her in Jakarta, I made the three-day journey out to that village in the middle of the jungle. When I got there, it appeared to be completely deserted except for a single, short, stooped old man who turned out to be completely illiterate.

"HelloIloveyou," he said in English, which was very weird. How does a unit of English language consisting of four words jammed together make it deep into the rainforests of Sumatra?

"Hello," I corrected him. "Just hello."

It turned out this was the only English he spoke. "HelloIloveyou," he repeated.

"Whatever," I answered. "Where are all the people?"

He said something in Indonesian I will never forget.

"*Mereka lagi di hutan berburu monyet.*" They again the forest to hunt the monkey.

"When will they return?" I asked.

He thought, then he answered, "Maybe tomorrow."

This "tomorrow" turned into more than two months, and still the only one I had ever seen in the village was that old man.

I didn't care. I hadn't gone there to teach English. I had gone there to love my girlfriend. I spent my days in the empty classroom composing beautiful letters with creative fantasies about our future together, full of erotic scenarios. I took to writing long contemplations about different parts of her body. I hit all the obvious ones right away—her hair, her eyes, her lips. Then I began to delve into those that were lesser known. In one letter I wrote, "How I long to dust with kisses the milky white skin of your breasts." Whether it was her breasts, her lips, her eyes, or her hair I was writing about, my standard closing became, "Oh, babe, you hold my beating heart in the palms of your hands."

Every week or so, a man with a horse arrived in the village. This was the Indonesian post office, and it was to him that I gave my letters, ten to twenty at a time. But in my time there, not a single letter ever came in return.

The old man was in charge of my well-being. He cooked every meal for me, he washed all of my clothes, he took me on walks through the jungle during which I would pick colorful flowers, which I pressed and added to the mail I sent my girlfriend—for effect.

Once I became extremely ill with a high fever. I don't know how many days I was sick, but the old man never left my side. He tended to me and nursed me back to health, and when I was strong again, that was when I decided I had to leave.

I packed my bags and I went to the old man. I told him I was lonely and depressed, and there were no students. There also seemed to be something wrong with the Indonesian post office because I really should have been receiving some letters back at this point. I turned to go find my girlfriend in Jakarta.

"HelloIloveyou," he said.

I turned back around. "HelloIloveyou," I said, and by that I meant goodbye.

It dawned on me how much in debt I was to the old man. What surprised me was how sad he seemed. Tears began to well in his eyes. I realized how lonely he must be, living in this village all by himself, and how much my presence must have meant to him.

At the flat in Jakarta where I had been sending my countless undying expressions of love, to my surprise, a large, red-faced man answered the door.

"Is my girlfriend here?" I asked.

"Huh? No!" He slammed the door in my face.

Well, I hadn't come all that way just to give up that easily, so I knocked again, but this time, I held up one of my letters. "Is my girlfriend here?" I pointed at the name on the envelope. His eyes widened in obvious recognition. He nodded his head and beckoned me through the door. He summoned his daughters, Mei Mei and Foo Foo, who were apparently studying English at school, and when they found out I was the one bombarding their house with this mail, they squealed with delight, and one of them shot off and returned with a large brown paper sack full of my letters.

In a feat of optimism, I kept expecting them to produce my girlfriend at any minute, that somehow she was living here with this family, but when they dumped my letters on the table and began to read parts out loud they had underlined, I began to grow despondent.

One of them began to read, "Oh, babe, you hold my beating heart in the palms of your hand," to which the other immediately responded, "How I long to dust with kisses the milky white skin"—she put her hand to her mouth and stifled a giggle—"of your breasts." They both shook with silent laughter. This was obviously a familiar routine around this house. What better way to learn English than by reading someone's bad love letters?

It was the father who eventually took pity on me and he phoned the landlord. He discovered that yes, before the family had moved in, my girlfriend had been there for about a week, but then she had left the country—with a Greek man. She had forgotten to do two things: one, tell me that she was leaving the country, and two, she had forgotten to break up with me! I had been stuck in the jungle sending dozens of letters to a girlfriend that existed, for the most part, only in my imagination!

Indeed, she had held my beating heart in her hand, but instead of honoring my devotion, my blind, naive devotion, instead of cherishing my heart, she had taken it and ripped it right out of my ass. It hurt. It still does.

As I stepped out of that flat in Jakarta, holding my heart, holding my ass, holding my sack of opened letters, I faced a decision.

I think it was in reaction to her betrayal that I decided to finish the contract I had signed. I think it was in reaction to her betrayal that I wanted to be loyal. And the only person in the world I had to be loyal to in that moment was that old man in that lonely village. It was to him that I returned. For the next three months or so, I spent every day with him.

I still spent days in the classroom, but instead of writing letters, I began to imagine what it would be like to have students. I began to write lesson plans. I still spent afternoons walking with the old man collecting flowers, but instead of pressing them and sending them off in the mail, I gave them names and placed them in the empty chairs of the classroom. They became my imaginary students. And this was my secret garden! You do strange things when you're in the jungle by yourself.

Then, one day, the man with the horse arrived, and there was a letter for me. It was from my organization. Based on my quarterly report that there were no students, they were closing this post in the jungle permanently and transferring me to a teaching position on the island of Bali. For a second time, I had to say goodbye to that old man.

I never heard from that girlfriend again, but it may surprise you to hear that every now and then I still sit down and write a letter out by hand. I have written about how in Bali, I met an Indonesian girl, fell in love, and got married. I've written about how after we moved to the United States, I ultimately ended up becoming a teacher. And those flowers that I placed in those empty chairs in that classroom in the middle of the jungle have actually transformed and become real students. I continue to feel like my classroom is my secret garden.

These letters are sent across the Pacific, where I suppose a man with a horse still picks them up and carries them deep into the rainforest to a lonely village where once, at least a long time ago, there lived an old man. I've never gotten a response, and I don't know if the man is still there or if he is even alive, but I'll never stop writing those letters.

I have signed every one of them, "HelloIloveyou."

Told at Coyote Tales
Schroeder Hall
Green Music Center
Rohnert Park, CA
September 16, 2018
For the video of this performance and others, visit
brandonspars.com

TELLING STORIES AROUND THE FIRE

*A*t the time this essay is being written, ten months have passed since the fires of October 9, 2017. Of course that is the day the fire started, and it wasn't until weeks later that it was finally put out. The fire burned around 40,000 acres, which is pretty typical for a wildfire, but this one entered Santa Rosa, California, and burned more than five thousand homes and buildings and killed more than twenty people. The community is still struggling to recover. You can still drive by fields of chimneys where houses once stood. You can still make someone wince with a careless comment such as "You were on fire during your presentation," or "Can I borrow the canoe that you keep in your garage?" And then the person whose house was burned has the difficult and absurd task of comforting you so you won't beat yourself up over your carelessness and crass ignorance.

I was asked to host part of a two-day event called "Thicker Than Smoke." This was an expression that was coined to capture the community spirit and the selfless and sometimes heroic efforts that the community made during and after the fires to rescue, comfort, and care for the victims of the fire. Love is thicker than smoke. Sonoma County met the tragic events with love. That was the idea.

And yet, the love could last only so long. After three weeks or so, the stacks of donated bottles of water began to disappear at the Santa Rosa Fairgrounds and on Kentucky Street in Petaluma. People had to jump back into their full-time jobs, and the drudgery of the mundane tasks such as answering emails that had stacked up or even returning overdue library books set back in for most.

This left those that had lost everything to begin dealing with insurance companies; rental units; the buying of new wardrobes, new cars, new paperclips, new hairbands, new glasses, and new dental floss. The mundane part of life became a monster in many ways more sinister and cruel than the fire-breathing dragon that had cut a swath of destruction right through their lives.

When I returned to teaching at Sonoma Academy after a week of campus closure, the list of students and faculty who had lost everything was crystal clear in my mind. But then, in that impersonal and indifferent passage of time, the list faded, and I began to make slips.

The worst was when I heard about a creative writing contest, and I immediately thought of my unstoppable freshman student Jennifer, who had not only written a story but a novel. She had printed the novel and made it into a six-volume set of books with hand-drawn illustrations. I rushed at her with the flyer for the contest and told her we could submit pictures of her drawings with the manuscript. She stared at me blankly. It had all burned six months earlier. Her computer had been incinerated, as had the backup hard drive. You can never be prepared for the speed and complete devastation of what was not actually a fire but a firestorm. It was a tornado of heat.

I knew that stare. It was the same stare as that of a student whom I scolded for not having the textbook—of course they had once had the textbooks, but they had burned. I began back-pedaling, and then I slipped into apologies. And then, of course, Jennifer began to comfort me. She told me a story.

"It's okay," she began. "I got to read it to the one that matters the most to me. For the last few weeks leading up to the fire, I read out loud to my father every night. I finished the entire thing just a few days before everything burned. If I had to choose a single person that I would have wanted to share it with, it would have been him."

She had given me a way out of my blunder. "Thank goodness," I said.

Maybe it was because of her ability to care for those who were trying to care about her loss that her name came immediately to my mind when I was trying to think of a young person to tell a story about the fire. I was in the audience at the premiere of *Urban Inferno* (a documentary about the October fire in Santa Rosa) when I overheard someone stating that they would like to know what the experience had been like for the young people—the children. And then I thought of her: Jennifer.

I didn't really know her fire story until she wrote it out and shared it with me. She had lived in a wealthy part of Santa Rosa known as Fountaingrove, and by the time she evacuated with her family, there were flames on both sides of the road. They met tourists who had been staying at a nearby hotel, and they pulled them in their car on the way down the hill, where the fire had just jumped Highway 101.

Jennifer's story had two very poignant moments. The first was in the parking lot of Target, which is where her family eventually landed after K-Mart burned. She had no idea what the fate of her house was, and a part of her believed strongly that it would be fine. She met up with her friend Kate, and they received news that Sophie, another classmate, had just lost her house.

"I don't know what to say to her," Jennifer said to Kate. "What can you say to someone who has just lost everything?"

What Jennifer didn't know was that she had just lost everything, too. She had the clothes she was wearing and that was all. When she presented her story at Weill Hall, a performing arts theater that is part of the Green Music Center at Sonoma State University, she wore the same jeans and t-shirt that she had had to live in for four days, until her family was settled enough in a hotel room to go shopping.

The second moment in the short, six-minute account was the ending of Jennifer's story. Weeks later, her family was let past the security checkpoint to look at their property, and they found a black, twisted wreck. Sitting right in the middle of it all, where their driveway used to be, was a shiny new trailer, which was where a security guard was stationed to protect the area from looters. They pondered what it would be like to live in the midst of the burnt remains of an entire neighborhood. They wondered if it was depressing to be surrounded with such devastation. But then, Jennifer's father made the comment, "I wouldn't rather be anywhere else." The family of four nodded. It was their home, after all. The father added, "Lucky guy."

I did not lose anything in the fires. At just before four in the morning on October 9, there was a pounding on my door. It was my neighbor Kashi, a construction manager who lived on the corner, two houses down. When I opened the door, he calmly told me I should probably evacuate because Santa Rosa was on fire. He licked his lips and gestured toward the red glow just north of us. The paleness of his face and the dryness of his mouth betrayed the calmness in his voice.

There was a strong, acrid smell of smoke—not the pleasant kind like a campfire but more like burning plastic or overheated car brakes. Within an hour, we were on the road in stopped traffic headed south on Highway 101. The only cars heading north into Santa Rosa were emergency vehicles, mostly ambulances. Five or six of them would barrel past in silence, lights flashing. The fact that they didn't have their sirens on was eerie, making it seem like some kind of long-term emergency had set in. And one had. We had to drive on the shoulder because the far left lane was being used by those same ambulances as they left Santa Rosa carrying patients evacuated from Sutter and Kaiser hospitals, which were both threatened by flames.

After three and a half hours, we made it to my parents' home in Marin, where we watched the news. Then the texts came rolling in from friends and colleagues—the names of families from Sonoma Academy whose homes were already gone.

We didn't stay away long. We were back home on Tuesday. Our neighborhood had not been officially evacuated, and it never was throughout the duration of the fires.

I began to spend time with three of the neighbors, all fathers. None of us were at work because of the fires, and we began to gather regularly on the corner in front of Kashi's house. We listened as Kashi read the Nixle emergency notification posts he received on his phone. Everything seemed like bad news.

"They're evacuating Crane Canyon Road," he read.

"Crap," Nick, a plumber, said.

"Damn," I, the teacher, added.

"No!" a neighbor by the name of AC, whom I was meeting for the first time, shouted. He installed floors as a profession. He was also the most restless. He paced around nervously as if in need of something to do. His wife and kids had remained in Petaluma when he, too, had been swept up by Kashi's Monday morning alarm. "We're not going down without a fight," he kept chanting, and then he glanced at the towers of smoke to the north and the east.

We took to patrolling the streets after Kashi read news of break-ins in a Nixle post. Most of the neighborhood seemed empty, probably because families wanted to keep their children away from the toxic air.

I was walking the far street on our block when Kashi texted, "Sketchy van!"

"Crap!" Nick texted.

"Damn!" I wrote, and I began to make my way towards our street. Curiously, there was no word from AC, but, as it turned out, there was a reason for that.

I had my son's baseball bat. Nick held a wrench that was the size of his leg, and Kashi arrived with something that looked like an insidious, medieval torture instrument. We stared at the device, which had a cutting edge but also a wire brush and something that looked like a chisel. "It's for cleaning my barbecue," he explained.

We all turned to the sketchy van.

It was red, dirty, and windowless. We couldn't tell if anyone was in it or not, so we crouched and made our way toward the driver's side. Just as Nick reached out to knock on the crusty side of the driver's door, Kashi straightened up. He was reading his phone.

"Hold up," he said. "The van belongs to AC's sister-in-law."

"Man," Nick exclaimed. "Why does she drive such a sketchy van?"

The next text from AC didn't answer the question, but

it sent all three of us home to our respective houses. AC informed us she had driven through fire to escape her burning home in Sonoma. She would be parking the van there indefinitely.

~

When the doors to Weill Hall were opened, three hundred people, each in a very different place in relation to the events of ten months prior, entered the theater. Many in the audience were first responders, a term that has come to include not only firefighters and law enforcement but also ambulance drivers, doctors, radio announcers, volunteers at shelters, and so many others. Many were victims of the fire, having lost everything they owned. And many, perhaps most, had not lost anything. For the two hours that followed, however, everyone was together in Weill Hall laughing, crying, and trying to help one another heal.

Our evening of stories began with a single spotlight on a rugged looking man in jeans. Tony Niel, Santa Rosa firefighter, narrated the events of October 8 and 9: how he had to evacuate from his own house, and then, once he was sure that his wife and children were safe, went into the station to see what could be done. He and his partner had driven through the smoke into the same neighborhood from which my student Jennifer had fled.

When you are a veteran firefighter, you develop a feeling, and Tony and his partner had a feeling that there still could be people trapped in the flaming neighborhood. Tony said he heard screams.

Tony stopped narrating. Dr. Judy Sakaki, the President

of Sonoma State University, joined Tony on the stage. Judy picked up the story where Tony left off.

Judy did not recall screaming for help. In her nightgown, barefoot, she was running aimlessly, holding the hand of her husband, trying any direction to escape the fire. But there was no way out. Their fire alarms hadn't awakened them, and nobody had knocked on their door to alert them. Now she was sure they were going to die. Then the headlights of Tony Niel's truck penetrated the smoke, and the truck drove over burning debris straight at her. Tony pulled Judy and her husband inside, and they made their way through flames and smoke out of the fire.

This was how "Thicker Than Smoke" began.

The event had been conceived by two prominent community members, Tom Birdsall of the Green Music Center Board and Nancy Lasseter. Their aim was to raise money for families of first responders who had lost their own homes while their loved ones were out fighting the flames threatening the homes of others. The star power of country music legends Brad Paisley and Bonnie Hunt, who performed the second night, ensured the event would bring in a lot of money from ticket sales, all of which was donated to the Community Resilience Fund.

Heading into the event, I couldn't help but feel a bit like an imposter. I didn't really feel like I had the right to share the stage with victims and first responders—but I believed in the project itself, which was to use story as a way to help the community heal. I knew that many stories about the heroic efforts of first responders had already been shared in the newspaper. I knew that victims had shared their stories with their close friends and in counseling. What hadn't happened was an evening in which individuals stood up and told their experiences in a formal and structured way to an audience.

As I had the honor of working with the storytellers prior to the event, I encouraged them to give their performances a clear beginning, middle, and end, and to shape their stories so they led up to a single moment, a climax, which was followed by a dénouement. As I worked with my student Jennifer, I could see how structuring her experiences in this way broke apart what had been a monstrous, terrifying, dismal, and raw experience into smaller units. She noticed how parts of her story contained irony and humor, not to mention hope and gratitude. These were different from the terror and confusion that had come to characterize any thought she had had about the events of October 9, 2017, and the months thereafter.

I was humbled by how receptive first responders and victims were to my approaching them not only to participate in the event but also to work with me on their stories. Without exception, the tellers opened themselves to me and my perspective, which was that of someone who had not suffered, and to my embarrassment, did very little in the way of helping others during this tragedy. In fact, when I reflected on the days I spent with Kashi, Nick, and AC, I began to conclude I was more a part of the problem than the solution.

Nick, the plumber, had made a run into his office, and when he returned, he had an enormous fire hose in the back of his truck. "About a hundred yards," he said proudly, and this got AC pumped up.

"Yes!" And then he said for the tenth time, "We ain't

going down without a fight." He shot a challenging look at the smoke rising behind Taylor Mountain.

Like four dads gathered around the grill at a pool party, we examined the fire hydrant that stood right on the corner in front of Kashi's house, and then Nick used the wrench that he had meant to be a weapon.

A beam of white water cut the brown air. Three of us held the hose as AC charged ahead, beckoning us to test the range of the hose. We hosed the roofs of houses on our block. We could even get the houses behind ours. The neighborhood began to drip. Water began to run in the gutters. Then we shot it over the field across the street from Kashi's house.

"If the fire's coming from anywhere, it's coming from this damn field," AC growled. "Let's soak it."

In the middle of the field stood a small house. At one time, there had been cattle not only in the field but also on the land where our homes had been built. A small Safeway sign was stuck to the side of the garage like a bumper sticker, but the cattle had been moved across Petaluma Hill Road for the Christopherson wave of tract homes, and a fence had been built along the boundary where Santa Rosa ended and Rohnert Park began.

The field was high with different grasses, which obscured the view of a pond that still lay sunk in the land from the days when cattle soaked there to escape the hundred-degree weather. I had often seen the rancher while walking my dog, but only from a distance as he drove his tractor around the field or worked sandblasting cars and repainting them. I don't know if I was too far away, but even though the bill of his hat was clearly turned toward me, he never returned my wave. Once while he was mowing right along the fence where bottles, cups, and McDonald's Happy Meal boxes collected, I made direct eye contact with him.

"Hello," I shouted. He stared at me indifferently. I told myself his tractor was too loud and he hadn't heard me.

"Ha ha!" AC shouted. He grabbed the firehouse and was aiming it at the small farmhouse. The rush of water, the hiss that it made, and the force it drove back gave us the feeling that we could fight. Of course, we hadn't seen the roaring wall of flames that jumped mountains and melted vehicles.

Not everyone had evacuated the neighborhood after all. Behind beads of water running from his eves, the rancher appeared.

For the first time I heard his voice. "What the hell are you doing?"

AC took a few steps toward him and put his hands on the top of the fence like he was going to climb it. Then he looked back at us.

Nick cranked the water off.

Kashi tried to sound official, "We're running some drills over here." He gestured to our block of homes, the rancher's former kingdom.

For the umpteenth time, AC stated, "We ain't going down without a fight." It sounded meek this time.

"Well, if you don't stop what you're doing, I'm going to call the sheriff." The rancher slammed his door.

Meanwhile, sheriff deputies and firefighters had a lot more important things to do than to respond to a call about four idiots using valuable water pressure.

To give a sense as to what it was like for the first responders, I only need reference Tom Siragusa's tale. A firefighter for forty-two years and Assistant Chief of the San Francisco Fire Department, Tom had arrived in Glen Ellen with his crew and hadn't stopped working for an entire week. With the Santa Rosa Fairgrounds completely swamped, he and his crew had nowhere to rest, shower, or eat. However, through a "soccer connection," he reached out to Chris Ziemer, Sonoma Academy's athletics director, and Tom and his crew of four trucks began staying in the school gym, where grateful parents brought food and toiletries for the physically exhausted crew.

At the "Thicker Than Smoke" event, Chris joined Tom on stage and stumbled for words and eventually broke down as he tried to describe Tom's crew, blackened with soot, swaying on their feet from exhaustion, but respectfully thanking him—thanking *him* for giving them a place to recuperate. Chris had been volunteering at the fairgrounds, but now shifted his attention to making sure this crew got everything they needed, including a round of cheers from parents and students every time they headed back out to fight the fires.

Not aware that our school was being used as a base-camp, I had taken students to a speech tournament, which we attended in spite of the fires, and I arrived very late Saturday night to return the van and the keys. As I walked down the dark hall, I suddenly stopped. I could hear the sound of heavy breathing at my feet, and then behind me as well. As my eyes adjusted I noticed shapes lining the hallway, and then through the open doors of the gym, I saw countless bodies stretched out on gym mats and blankets.

The foil trays of food I had passed suddenly made sense, and then I blundered into a butcher paper banner. In the style used for announcing big lacrosse or soccer games, the banner read, "Welcome San Francisco Fire!" and "You are home right here!" and "Thank you!" and "We love you."

I felt something I have never felt before. I teach ancient literature, and I have read Homer with my students for years. There are scenes from the Trojan War when the heroes stumble back from the battlefield to lose themselves "in the long arms of sleep," their deep breathing coming from every tent. For a moment, I felt like I was privileged to a glimpse, an omniscient one, of humanity expended to its very limits—greatness rebuilding.

I was completely surrounded by more than two dozen dozing heroes. With them all breathing in unison like one being of gigantic stature, I knew the fire, wherever it was, didn't stand a chance. To say that they are professional is not quite correct. The stereotype of a professional is someone who is calm and doesn't break a sweat. They go home at the end of the day. They know how to handle every situation. These firefighters truly shattered that mold.

If I hadn't had this private vision, or if I hadn't had the opportunity to meet firefighters like Tony Niel or Tom Siragusa, I don't know if I ever would have appreciated how much of a parody the three other dads and I were as we went about our patrolling of the neighborhood and our preparatory drills.

The climax of the week of fire came for us late in the week when smoke began pouring up from behind Taylor Mountain. We were gathered on the corner in front of

Kashi's when he pointed at the column of white smoke mixed with black, which seemed to rise right out of the hill itself, giving it the appearance of a volcano.

"Crap!" Nick snapped.

"Damn!" I grumbled.

AC gripped his head and howled, "No!"

That was when we heard buzzing. Across the field we saw a line of men, each of them swinging a weed-eater.

"What the hell?" Kashi murmured.

It just so happened that we weren't the only makeshift neighborhood squad around. A group of about ten men had come over the fence from the other side clearly with the intention of cutting down the entire field.

Kashi had already hopped our side of the fence and was marching over toward them. We watched as he stood in front of one of the men. Kashi waved his arms. The man swept his hand as if to indicate the dimensions of the field. Kashi pointed at the rancher's house. Then he marched back toward us.

"They've lost their minds," Kashi began.

AC piped, "Those weed-eaters are gonna catch the field on fire!"

"That's just what they want to do. They're going to do a backburn!"

"No, they ain't!" AC shouted in the direction of the men.

Kashi continued. "Look at them. One of them's squirting the place they're cutting with lighter fluid."

"Holy crap," I muttered.

AC was really fired up. "Come on, boys!" He held a ring of keys in his hand and he gestured at the burnt red van that belonged to his sister-in-law. He looked at Nick. "We can mount the hose right on top!"

Nick shook his head. "Goddamn!" He went over to the fire hydrant and picked up his enormous wrench.

Nick and I fed hose while Kashi nosed the red van into the gate towards the rancher's house. He turned off and came through the field alongside the fence. AC climbed on top of the van and held the fire hose at his hip like a weapon. He gave a signal with his arm, and Nick cranked down on the wrench. The white beam shot up into the brown air.

We heard the men with weed-eaters at the other end shouting. AC aimed the hose right at them, and Kashi began to guide the van slowly through the brush in their direction.

"I'm gonna hose 'em right back over their side of the fence!" AC shouted.

Of course, AC did not hose the men. The men never lit the rancher's field on fire. The climax of this neighborhood tale never went any further, because this time the rancher *did* phone the sheriff, and an exhausted deputy arrived. No backburn! No fire hose! We were all guilty of adding to the problem and creating more work! Next time we would all be cited!

Ten months later, in Weill Hall, the climax was told by husband and wife Josh Weil and Claire Mollard. Josh was the Assistant Chief Medical Officer at Kaiser Permanente, which was eventually evacuated. Josh and Claire performed a duo telling of their harrowing night.

After a consultation with his wife, Josh had gone down the hill from their home in Fountaingrove where he stepped into a situation that was rapidly becoming a total emergency. Throughout Josh's decision to evacuate the entire hospital and Claire's frantic escape from the "roaring wall of fire" that was sweeping down on her house, they were connected by fragile and fading cell reception. At one point the phone was handed to Josh's ninth-grade daughter, Sophie, who couldn't stop screaming, and as Josh issued orders directing busloads of patients and ambulances carrying those from intensive care out of the hospital and away from the flames approaching from Wikiup, he intermittently tried to comfort his distraught daughter. "Mommy was trying to find the cat," was all he knew, and then she was back on the line driving their car through fire. Eventually the line went dead as the cell towers themselves were engulfed in the inferno.

Claire was reliving the events as she performed them for the audience. With tears streaming down her face, as her family was reunited in a parking lot, she said over and over, "We were alive. We were alive, and that's all that mattered. We were alive!"

For so many, cell phones had been the only thread connecting them with those they loved, and as the cell towers burned one by one, the digital fibers that held them together disintegrated and were gone.

In the style of Moth StorySLAMs, between the stories, we read slips of paper that had been filled out by members of the audience. We got a sense for the diverse experiences that members of the audience had during the fire. The prompt read: "I knew we were going off the script for anything I had ever experienced before when…"

Some of the responses were humorous.

I knew we were going off the script for anything I had experienced when...

- members of my family seriously considered going into the bomb shelter on our property. (It is dominated by mold.)
- I was evacuating in my motorhome headed for the coast on Hwy. 12 when I realized that someone had siphoned off my gas and my tank was almost empty.
- [after we lost our home] we were offered a rental at $6,500.00 per month and thought, "What a bargain!"

Many objectively reported what had happened.

I knew we were going off the script for anything I had experienced when...

- I saw a bright red horizon filled with smoke while finding huge pieces of ash all over our property.
- we heard the fire jumped Hwy. 101 and K-Mart was on fire. The radio said Fountaingrove was gone. Two of my friends who lived just blocks away saw their homes catch fire.
- I stepped out onto the deck at 1:00 am and saw that the entire ridge was a wall of flames. As wide as I could see—roaring, whipping flames.

And then there were a couple that brought the evening to complete silence.

I knew we were going off the script for anything I had experienced when...

- I woke up and smelled smoke at 1:30 am that fateful day all the way up in Cloverdale—the very time my daughters-in-law most likely perished in the fire, behind Cardinal Newman. It was sadly confirmed the next morning when there was no sign of them at any shelters or hospitals. They were the second and third confirmed casualties. May we erect an honorary edifice for all those who were lost.
- my mom called and told me her house was on fire and she couldn't get out. Her last words to me were, "I'm going to die."

Seventeen people perished in the fires, and in more than a few of the cases, their loved ones were on the phone with them in their last moments. In some cases, as was reported by *The Press Democrat*, they were on the phone with 911 dispatchers who could only tell them that it was unlikely help was coming and that all they could do was try to escape.

One thing the 911 dispatchers never did was hang up on them, and, as it was reported, they stayed on the line until there was only silence. The dispatchers continued to talk to these victims even when they were screaming in agony, to comfort them so that they would know they weren't alone, all the way to the point where the phones lines burned or the cell towers failed.

Santa Rosa is like anywhere else. We curse at one another after being cut off in traffic, we grumble when someone is taking too long at the checkout line in the supermarket, and we complain to our servers in restaurants when our food is cold and then cut their tips to show our dissatisfaction. I believe we are like anywhere else in another sense, too.

In an emergency, we will stop to pull one another into the safety of our cars, even when we have never met; we will reach out to those who are exhausted with no place to sleep; over the radio and over the phone we will soothe and comfort one another with limitless energy, concern, and compassion, and we will never give up on one another. We have shown we are willing to drive back into fire to make sure everybody is safe. We have shown that we are willing to stay with one another on the line all the way to the very end.

As we told our stories under the event title "Thicker Than Smoke," Santa Rosa was already in the process of "Rising from the Ashes," another popular theme around the fires that was famously painted on a driveway in front of the ruins of a burned home.

One of the tellers, Katy Mangan, had returned to her home on Sonoma Mountain to find it turned to ash. It had been completely incinerated, all except for a single object. Sitting in the middle of the charred remains was a stone statue of the Buddha, which she took and placed in the passenger seat of her car. It was all she had of her former life; it became her constant companion as she drove from place to place and eventually resettled in town; it helped her learn to let go of all of the things she had once owned in her life and to heal each time her heart was cracked open by a memory or a comment someone made.

Katy described the statue in her story. The stone had been blasted by the incinerating forces of the firestorm, and its surface had changed. Once dark, shiny stone, it had blossomed from within as if by those very tectonic forces that move the crust of our earth, filling the stone with tiny cracks and faults, changing it forever into something, as Katy quoted from Shakespeare's *The Tempest*, "rich and strange."

The feeling now is that Santa Rosa will forever have a fault or divide. There will be "before the fire" and "after the fire." And the "fire change" Katy describes her statue having undergone is continuing to occur.

If one drives up River Road, which was badly burned, you no longer look for the blackened places to know where the fire had been. Ironically, it is those places that are the most green with new lush vegetation that were the most badly burned.

Of course, slowly but surely, the same is happening to neighborhoods as brand new homes go up where older ones were lost. And maybe one day, evidence of the fires will only be contained in private possessions like Katy's statue—and, of course, the memories and grief of those who went through it. This is why we need to continue to tell our stories.

When we tell stories formally, in front of a live audience, we move our personal, individual, specific experiences into a collective realm where healing can take place.

Of course, we can do this when we write our stories as well, but there is still a difference. When a teller faces an audience, there is an immediate risk not present in the act of writing and reading. This risk, I believe, makes all the difference.

This risk is what keeps many people off the stage altogether; and indeed, as I worked with many of the tellers at the "Thicker Than Smoke" event, there was a great deal of trepidation leading up to standing on the big stage at Weill Hall. But for every single individual who stood there and told their story, the power that was greater than the fear of public speaking was the desire and the need to tell their story.

Standing at the doors with the sound crew, awaiting the signal to walk out, the teller is alone and feels completely cut off from the audience, which takes on the proportions of an entire society. The audience can even feel like somewhat of an adversarial presence, full of the same kind of judgment that I felt from my mother, discussed in the introduction to this volume.

These tellers walked onto the stage, and in some cases began with trembling voices as they experienced a level of stress much higher than when talking to a friend about these tragic events. This is when the magic can happen. In most cases, aside from rowdy comedy clubs, the audience is already sympathetic to the speaker because of the risk that they are taking. Unlike a writer who is creating a main character, struggling to make them likable to the reader, the person on the stage, shaky voice and all, has already impressed the audience with their bravery and their willingness to open themselves up. A connection starts to form.

I think of my student Jennifer, who explained how her parents had seemed so casual and nonchalant when she showed them her friend's text about the approaching fires. The audience may have surprised her with their laughter when she rolled her eyes and grumbled that they never took anything she or her friends said seriously, and she had to stop as the laughter rolled through the theater. And when she arrived at the closing of her story, as her father reflected on how lucky the security guard was to be living right where they yearned to be, on their land, Jennifer saw tears in the eyes of the audience. She was reliving her experience, but she was reliving it with three hundred people. She saw that that she could share in the very power of the fire and transform its ferocious energy into a force that moved others, which was empowering for her. At the very least, she had appropriated some of power of the experience.

And just as Jennifer was being transformed, so was the audience.

Every mention of the 911 dispatchers who refused to go home and stayed even though their shifts were over, who stayed on the line with individuals even though they had been handed slips of paper from their superiors telling them that no help would arrive for that individual, the dispatchers who repeated, "I am still here... I am still with you... You aren't alone..." to those that were alone facing the flames, that is what the audience became the night of our event. The fragile thread that connected these dispatchers to the victims was connecting each member of the audience to the one telling their story, and in that way the teller was reassured by three hundred people: "We are here with you... you are not alone... what you went through was harrowing... we will never forget you."

Thicker Than Smoke
Weill Hall
The Green Music Center, Sonoma State University
Rohnert Park, CA
August 3, 2018
For a brief video synopsis of this event, visit
brandonspars.com

PART III
THE CLASSROOM

USING STORIES AND STORYTELLING
IN THE CLASSROOM

Here are some ways to use this book in the classroom. These activities work both for language classrooms, including ESL and literature, and classrooms devoted to the performance aspects of storytelling. The fourth suggestion is geared toward the deployment of storytelling to aid in recovery and healing. As mentioned in the description of this activity, you should consider providing counseling at any storytelling event that is devoted to healing as a community in the face of tragedy.

1. STORIES WE TELL

Discussion questions

In the introduction to this volume, the author discusses casual storytelling at the family dinner table. Are there times when you tell stories, even brief ones? When was the last time that you told a brief story? Who was it to? Can you think of a time when you told a longer, more detailed story? What was the story?

Tasks

1. Choose a story you have told recently and develop it by adding details and giving it a story structure with a beginning, middle, and end.
2. In the introduction, the author describes how he embellished the stories to make them more captivating for his mother. What would you do to your story to make it more engaging?

2. SELF-DISCOVERY

Discussion questions

In the first two tales in this book, "A Big Night Out" and "Secret Garden," the teller learns something about himself. What would you say the lesson was in each case?

Task

Think of a time that you learned something about yourself—a like or dislike, a deep fear you didn't know you had, a family trait you bear, a hidden skill or talent that suddenly manifested itself—and prepare a brief story about it. Try to give your narrative a beginning, middle, and an end. Be sure to link your story to the theme, "Self-Discovery"!

3. READING AND SUMMARIZING

Tasks

Before reading the third chapter, "Telling Stories Around the Fire":

Learn about the events. *The Press Democrat* received a Pulitzer Prize for their extensive coverage of the Tubbs and Atlas Fires. The Sonoma State paper, *The Star*, also included some excellent coverage.

1. Browse through the articles from *The PD* and *The SSU Star* at the following links:

- hyperurl.co/0pxz7f
- hyperurl.co/7rimdz
- hyperurl.co/t4shbf
- hyperurl.co/xtd64a
- hyperurl.co/plv7g2
- hyperurl.co/g6k4d6

2. Work in groups to summarize the basic information about the October Fires. Where and when did the fires start? Why did they spread so quickly? Where did they burn?

3. Based on the news coverage you have read, describe the stories and the storytellers you expect might have participated in the event, "Thicker Than Smoke"? After reading the third chapter, decide whether there were there any voices that seemed to be missing.

4. THE TELLER AND THEIR AUDIENCE

Reflection

In the third chapter, "Telling Stories Around the Fire," the audience plays an important role in the potential for healing tellers who have experienced trauma. Consider these questions:

- What are signs an audience would give a teller to indicate that they are being supportive?
- What is their posture like?
- What are their facial expressions like?

Tasks

Practice being a supportive, nurturing audience while a teller/student shares a brief story.

What would the opposite of this kind of audience be? Stone-faced? Scowling? This can be quite scary to do, but try having a teller/student perform a story to an audience that does *not* support them. (Avoid being outright antagonistic by shouting or throwing things—even wadded paper!)

5. TELLING STORIES AROUND THE FIRE

Discussion, Reflection, and Task

The chapter "Telling Stories Around the Fire" included several responses to the prompt

I knew we were going off the script for anything I had ever experienced before when...

Look back over those if you want, but below are other responses that weren't included in the chapter. What do you learn about the person writing the response? Who are they? A student? A medical worker? A father or mother or grandparent? Imagine a story for one of these responses. Where does the response fit into the story? At the beginning? The middle? The end? If you want, try briefly telling your version of the story. Here are some other responses to work with:

1. I went outside because it looked like it was snowing. It wasn't snow but burnt pages. I could tell the pages were all from the Bible. They must have been those Bibles from the bedside drawers in the hotel that burned.

2. I went to bed expecting to lazily and unwillingly drag myself out of bed to go to school in the morning, but instead [I was awakened] in the middle of the night by my mom [telling] me we need to leave.

3. I awoke to a smoky neighborhood in South Windsor with neighbors gathered on the sidewalk discussing what to do. We packed up the car, and waited. The internet stopped working. The cell phones didn't work. We didn't know whether to stay or go. Where was the fire? We felt anxious. Finally, my friend pulled out a radio you could power by winding it up. Never have I been so thankful for a radio's time-tested technology. Finally, we could figure out what was going on.

4. I realized my gas tank was empty… and it was impossible to make it to Redwood Valley Station.

I left my car and got in with my wife [who was driving our other car.]

5. I looked out the fourth floor window of Kaiser as I was helping evacuate patients, and there was fire—very close big fire—in every direction I could see. Then I knew why the police had asked us to "step it up."

6. We realized that the house where my son and his family had [once] lived on Heights Road was destroyed. Our son [had] died January 4, 2017. One layer of grief upon another.

7. When I got an automated message from Sonoma Academy saying multiple fires were burning in the North Bay and school was closed. They told us to be safe.

8. Our neighbor called at 2:15 am on our landline on Monday, October 9 and said, "We have to evacuate! The fire is close!"

9. Sitting with our friends at a bakery in Kenwood in March. Three firetrucks drove by, and we all jump!

10. Being at Mt. Lassen last week, smelling the smoke from the awful Carr Fire in the Redding Area, realizing and remembering all the anxiety, fear, and stress (PTSD) from the October fires.

11. I was regrouping in my car at a church after being evacuated and someone stole one of the transport vans from Fountaingrove and backed up at high speed—narrowly missing my car and smashing four other cars on his way out of the parking lot. We all just stood and stared…

12. We pulled embers the size of dinner plates off the roof of Sonoma State University's academic buildings. We had to send the University Police Department out on ember patrols.

13. I got a 911 call from my neighbor at 4 AM to please come home. He needed help loading horses into trailers. Everything north of Hopper was on fire. I asked about my mom's house, [and] he said check the news. Her house was on fire on the news...

6. YOUR COMMUNITY

Task

Think about an event in your community or at your school that you and your classmates could tell stories about. It could be something tragic and sad, like a natural disaster or an emergency you all experienced.

When the "Thicker Than Smoke" event was held, there were several volunteer counselors on site to talk to members of the audience if they began to feel over-whelmed. If you and your class choose to do something that involves trauma, you may want to consider discussing this with your school counselor and making them available when you perform your stories.

Be sure to spend time crafting your story. Give it a beginning, middle, and end. Notice parts of the story where there are different tones: humor, irony, sadness, terror, grief, joy. This was a very important part of the process in the "Thicker Than Smoke" event.

Also consider telling stories about an event that wasn't

tragic, such as a big sports victory or a school retreat/field trip. Whether a tragic event or not, be sure to brainstorm important facts and details about your event. Consult newspapers, radio, and video if they are available so that your personal experiences can be told within a frame that is accurate and grounded in fact.

ABOUT THE AUTHOR

 Brandon Spars lived and traveled in Indonesia and the Pacific Islands for about six years before attending the University of California, Berkeley, to earn his Master of Arts in Southeast Asian Studies and his Ph.D. in Interdisciplinary Studies. Since then, Brandon has taught high school and college for more than twenty years.

The classroom has always been his storytelling laboratory where loud booms, bellows, whoops, and thumps are frequently heard. Two years ago, Brandon began taking his stories outside the classroom to compete in events such as the Moth StorySLAM. He won the Moth GrandSLAM held in San Francisco in April 2016 with his story "Leaps," included in the first volume of *Live to Tell*.

Brandon lives with his wife and two children in Santa Rosa, California.

CPSIA information can be obtained
at www.ICGtesting.com
Printed in the USA
LVHW041450100719
623686LV00001B/116